I0004562

Nikolaos Karagiannis

The Future with Mobatest Corporation

It is my personal vision that created Mobatest Corporation.

For the cration of technological breakthroughs ,like wireless electricity,a hat with electrodes that will connect the brain with the computer,the cellphone and the video game console.

My corporation will create 22 core microprocessors for laptops and mainframes.

I will invent electric charge systems from satellites.

Semiconductros for spaceships.

22 parallel processing
microprocessors.

The future world will be like the Star Wars movie and the world of the William Gibson movies.

I will create microchips that will send electronic signals to the brain and body to improve human health.

Chips created from Mobatest Corporation will increase the gigabit that travel through optic fibres.

Semiconductors created by Mobatest will create antigravity and propulsion for vehicles like cars that everyone uses every day.

Customers of Mobatest
Corporation will include
Intel,AMD,Sony,Apple and the
telecommunication sector.

We design semiconductors and
microchips for many different
sectors of the economy.

Mobatest Corporation with my personal guidance will create microchips that will send images inside the brain with new implants and new chips created with nanotechnology.

Customers of Mobatest Corporation will be the telecom,wireless communications laptop and video game console industries.Mobile phones and tablets will use microchips designed by Mobatest Corporation and manufactured by companies like Intel,AMD and Chinese-Taiwanese manufacturers of microchips.

We design the best microchips in the market and we use special mathematical optimization algorithms to build the best semiconductors ever.

With the braintrust I have assembled in the Mobatest Corporation group of people we can create the best semiconductors ever created and we use the best software in the market to create them.

We have patents for hundreds of different microchips for many different industries.

My name is Nikolaos Karagiannis.I am the founder,president,chief executive officer and inventor of Mobatest Corporation.I am also the chief technology officer for Mobatest.

I have a university degree in
Computer Engineering,a
university degree in economics
and a degree in journalism.

www.ingramcontent.com/pod-product-compliance
Lightning Source LLC
Chambersburg PA
CBHW060938050326
40689CB00013B/3148